MELVIL DEWEY

Publishing Pioneers

MELVIL DEWEY

LIBRARY GENIUS

by Jill Sherman

Content Consultant:
Wayne A. Wiegand, F. William Summers Professor of Library and
Information Studies and Professor of American Studies
Florida State University, Tallahassee, Florida

ABDO
Publishing Company

CREDITS

Published by ABDO Publishing Company, 8000 West 78th Street, Edina, Minnesota 55439. Copyright © 2010 by Abdo Consulting Group, Inc. International copyrights reserved in all countries. No part of this book may be reproduced in any form without written permission from the publisher. The Essential Library™ is a trademark and logo of ABDO Publishing Company.

Printed in the United States.

♻ PRINTED ON RECYCLED PAPER

Editor: Mari Kesselring
Copy Editor: Sarah Frigon
Interior Design and Production: Nicole Brecke
Cover Design: Nicole Brecke

Library of Congress Cataloging-in-Publication Data
Sherman, Jill.
  Melvil Dewey : library genius / by Jill Sherman.
     p. cm. — (Publishing pioneers)
  Includes bibliographical references and index.
  ISBN 978-1-60453-761-1
  1. Dewey, Melvil, 1851-1931—Juvenile literature. 2. Librarians—United States—Biography—Juvenile literature. I. Title.
  Z720.D5S54 2009
  020'.92—dc22
  [B]
                                        2009009995

TABLE OF CONTENTS

The Dewey Decimal Classification system helps people locate books in libraries.

CLASSIFICATION

Imagine entering your school library and finding a book on astronomy shelved next to a history text. Near those, you find books on horses, Judaism, poetry, and China. You would probably be confused and frustrated that you cannot find the book you are looking for. This situation might seem strange, but in the early nineteenth century, library books were often shelved in such a seemingly haphazard way.

For a long time, librarians shelved books this way without much of a problem. Libraries were smaller, and because books were expensive, they could afford fewer books than today's libraries. When librarians added a new book to the collection, they would assign that book a spot on one of the shelves where there was room for it. Whatever new books the library obtained were easy to keep track of because the library did not have that many books.

But by the mid-nineteenth century, books were much cheaper to produce, and libraries were growing rapidly. The old system would not work any longer. A new system of classification was needed.

Importance of Libraries

A library is a collection of books or other published material that is preserved and organized. Most modern libraries house books, magazines, newspapers, maps, CDs, films, and computer systems. Other libraries are specialized. These libraries may house rare books, manuscripts, works of art, or specialized information in a given area of study, such as medicine.

Libraries give people access to knowledge. They allow people to study and do research. They also help people learn about a hobby and read for pleasure. Some libraries have special programs for patrons of all ages, such as lectures or children's story hours.

Libraries also help people learn about their communities. Through libraries, they can find out how to access government resources they might not have known were available.

FINDING A SOLUTION

How to classify, or group, books on the shelves was one of the biggest problems that librarians faced in the mid-nineteenth century. Several classification systems were used, but they had flaws.

Melvil Dewey, an assistant librarian at Amherst College in Massachusetts, was especially concerned with the problem. Frustrated with the inefficiency of the systems used at Amherst, Dewey began researching other methods. Dewey identified strengths and weaknesses in all the systems he investigated. Dewey was a driven and very ambitious

A History of Libraries

The first libraries served as archives of public records. In Mesopotamia, an ancient civilization in present-day Iraq, libraries housed records marked on clay tablets. These tablets were incredibly durable, and a number of them survive today.

At the same time in Egypt, records were written on papyrus scrolls. Papyrus is an early form of paper made from the papyrus plant. Though much less durable than clay, some of these papyrus scrolls still survive. The Alexandrian Library in Egypt once held the world's greatest collection of scrolls. But the library and all its contents were destroyed over the centuries.

Paper, invented in China approximately 2,000 years ago, is best suited for bookmaking. Once the printing press was invented in the fifteenth century, books could be made more cheaply, and libraries began to grow. Universities and libraries spread across Europe during the seventeenth and eighteenth centuries. Many early libraries were reserved for government use. In England, public libraries became popular by the late nineteenth century.

man. He was not satisfied with using an imperfect system.

Dewey soon realized that he would have to design his own system of classification. This system would classify a wide range of subjects and also allow for the addition of new subjects presently unknown. His was a difficult task. Dewey considered the challenge for months, reading about every system of book arrangement that he could.

At last, an idea occurred to him:

I dreamed night and day that there must be a satisfactory solution . . . one Sunday during a sermon . . . the solution flasht over me so that I jumpt in my seat and came very near shouting "Eureka!" Use decimals to number a classification of all human knowledge in print.[1]

Dewey's system combined the best parts of those systems already in use. But his plan merged these systems together to suit any library. Dewey divided all knowledge into nine main categories (which has become ten in today's updated version of the classification system). Each of these categories was assigned a number. For example, science is classified in the 500s. Science is a broad topic, however. Narrower science topics were assigned more specific numbers under the 500s grouping. For example, physics is classified in the 530s. Magnetism, a subset of physics, is in the 538s. As the subject is defined more narrowly, additional decimals can place a book in its precise category. Then, books with the same numbers are shelved alphabetically by the author's last name.

According to library historian Matthew Battles,

Thus [Dewey] joined the analytical simplicity of decimal numbers to an intuitive scheme of knowledge, one that would fluidly accommodate all the books ever written, and all the books that could be written as well.[2]

Dewey promptly implemented the system at Amherst's library. Soon, other librarians recognized the merits of the Dewey Decimal Classification (DDC). Eventually, the system would become standard in public and school libraries across the United States and around the world. In fact, the DDC would become the most widely used system of organizing library books. As of 2009, it was used in more than 200,000 libraries worldwide. And in the United States, the DDC was used in about 95 percent of all school and public libraries. The DDC has been revised many times in order to keep

Melvil Dewey developed the Dewey Decimal Classification system.

up with modern technology and new areas of study. Since Dewey's original version of the system was established in 1876, the DDC had been revised 22 times, as of 2009.

MAKING A BETTER LIBRARY

Although Dewey is best known for his classification system, his influence on modern libraries is much more far-reaching. Dewey strove to improve all aspects of library operation. He knew that librarians would need special education.

Many school and public libraries separate fiction and nonfiction books. However, this practice does not strictly follow the Dewey Decimal Classification (DDC). Literature is classified in the 800s in the DDC. However, works of fiction are very popular among library patrons. And because such a large number of fiction works are published each year, librarians often separate fiction and nonfiction books. This makes finding books easier and avoids having a large number of shelves devoted to the 800s.

Dewey established a school for the education of librarians, and he helped found the American Library Association (ALA). He also started the Library Bureau, a company that sold standardized furniture and office supplies for libraries. Dewey wanted all libraries to use his specially designed supplies. As Battles says,

> Dewey was thinking about libraries every-where . . . he hoped libraries would be established in even the smallest communities to serve the most marginal populations. He really had a single, ideal library in mind.[3]

Dewey's focus on reform extended to areas beyond libraries. He was an active proponent of the metric system and spelling reform in the United States. Dewey approached every area of reform with enthusiasm and vigor. He focused on organization and efficiency, sometimes to the distress of his coworkers. But despite their opposition, Dewey's work made a lasting impression on libraries and education that can still be seen today.

Melvil Dewey

Like many families in upstate New York during the mid-1800s, the Deweys supported women's rights and other types of reform.

A Desire to Reform

The mid-nineteenth century was a time of political and religious reform in the United States. Upstate New York, in particular, was home to many with strong convictions regarding religion, abolitionism (opposition to slavery), women's rights, and education reform, among other controversial issues of the time. It was in this environment that Melville Dewey was born and raised.

Joel and Eliza Dewey settled in Adams Center, a village in upstate New York, shortly after their marriage. They raised five children, Marion, Manfred, Marietta, Marissa, and Melville. Melville (who later changed the spelling of his name to Melvil) was youngest, born on December 10, 1851.

A RELIGIOUS FAMILY

The Deweys belonged to the Adams Seventh Day Baptist Church. But in 1852, when controversy arose about the church's beliefs, Joel and Eliza both broke away from their place of worship. However, the couple did not agree on what changes in theology needed to be made. Joel and Eliza then became prominent members of separate

The Burned-Over District

Adams Center was located in Jefferson County, New York, in the northwestern part of the state. This area had been swept by religious reform and revival many times between 1800 and 1850. As a result, the region came to be known as the "Burned-Over District" because each religion would eventually burn out and a new one would come in. This process was repeated over and over. Religious groups that found a home in this region include Charles Gradison Finney's evangelical Christians, Mormons, Millerites, Shakers, Fourierists, and Oneida perfectionists. In addition, social issues such as abolition, temperance (opposition to alcohol consumption), education reform, and women's rights were often discussed and advocated by the people of the Burned-Over District.

congregations. Their children attended both of their parents' choices. On Saturday, they attended church with their mother, and on Sunday they went to their father's church. Eventually, the time came for the Dewey children to decide which church to join. All but Melville chose to be baptized in their mother's church.

The fact that the Dewey family worshiped in two different churches does not appear to have caused any problems within the family. If anything, it may have helped

The Baptist Church

Baptists emerged in England during the early seventeenth century and are a subset of a larger Protestant group. They oppose baptism for infants, reserving the ritual for adults, who they feel are mature enough to understand its significance. Baptists believe that individuals are free to choose any religion, to make their own decisions in matters of faith, and to interpret the Bible themselves.

Baptist churches are not governed by a central organization. When a congregation is established, its founding members determine the set of beliefs the members will follow. For this reason, most Baptist churches vary somewhat in their beliefs. The Seventh Day Baptists observe the Sabbath, or day of rest, on Saturday. Saturday was originally the seventh day of the week. So, Seventh Day Baptists believe the Sabbath should be celebrated then.

Some Baptist churches also believe in the "second coming" of Jesus Christ. William Miller shared this belief with his followers, the Millerites. Miller predicted that the second coming and the end of the world would occur in 1843. His followers were deeply disappointed when the world did not end that year, and many broke away to form their own churches. Some of these churches maintained that a second coming was sure to happen, but they did not predict when it would occur.

strengthen the importance of religion in their lives. Joel and Eliza Dewey were known to be two of the hardest-working people in town. Likewise, their children were hardworking, serious, and responsible. Both parents opposed liquor and tobacco and supported moral reform in church and at home.

The Deweys also praised stoicism, or keeping one's feelings in control, and humility of character. The Dewey children took these teachings to heart. As a result, Melville's childhood was marked by a certain loneliness. Though he was always surrounded by family, young Melville sometimes felt as though his home lacked warmth and affection. He once wrote to his brother, "I often regret exceedingly, that there was never much affection manifested in our immediate family."[1]

The Civil War

Melville Dewey was ten years old at the start of the American Civil War (1861–1865). At this time, the issue of slavery was very controversial. Many in the North believed it was wrong and should be outlawed. In the South, slavery helped plantations thrive, and many people did not wish to see it outlawed. Southern states began to secede from the United States, creating their own Confederate States of America. U.S. president Abraham Lincoln declared the war to preserve the Union.

The war was fought mainly in the South, far from the Deweys' home in New York. Though Melville's feelings about the war were not well recorded, he may have sided with the North. He attended a rally for Lincoln prior to his election on November 1, 1860.

DETERMINING HIS LIFE'S WORK

Like other children his age, Melville liked ice skating, hiking, hunting, and fishing. He had chores to do on the weekends, and he sometimes helped out with the family's businesses. The Deweys owned six properties in Adams Center, New York. Three of these properties were stores, which served as a source of income for the family. The family's most profitable store, and the one that served as their primary source of income, made and sold shoes and boots. Melville's mother worked in this shop, sewing some of the shoes by hand.

As a child, Melville took his education seriously. Self-education was an important part of building character in young men during this era. Melville was a voracious reader. He could spend hours each day lying on the floor with his nose in a book. At age 13, he walked to Watertown, a town ten miles (16 km) from Adams Center, to buy himself a Webster's unabridged dictionary.

But Melville was also different from many of his peers. As a teenager, Melville became obsessed with deciding what his life's work would be. He spent hours alone, considering his destiny. He wanted his life to make a difference.

Melville walked ten miles (16 km) to Watertown to buy a dictionary

After much thought, Melville decided to dedicate his life to reform. He then purchased a set of cufflinks and had them inscribed with the letter *R*. According to Melville, the cufflinks would serve as "a constant reminder . . . that I was to give my life to reforming certain mistakes and abuses."[2]

Melville considered entering the field of education. As a teacher, he would be in a good position to influence reform. So, during the summer of 1867, Melville began taking steps to improve his own education. That winter, he began taking classes at the Adams Collegiate Institute.

While at the Adams Collegiate Institute, Melville helped organize a group called Young People's Lyceum. Little is known about the group's activities. However, it is known that Melville was the editor of the group's journal. Melville used the journal to discuss issues that needed reform. In its pages, he argued that the United States should adopt the metric system of weights and measures. He also criticized alcohol consumption.

UNSTOPPABLE

In January 1868, a fire broke out at the Adams Collegiate Institute. Seventeen-year-old Melville was at the school when the fire began. He responded by entering the smoke-filled building and carrying as many books as he could to safety. When the fire became too intense to continue,

Efficiency

Melville had little patience for wasting time. He believed that organization and efficiency improved society by helping people make the best use of their time. As such, his education reform focused on improving efficiency. Melville believed that students could learn twice as fast.

Melville was also critical of the Protestant churches. He thought they wasted too much time focusing on minor differences among different sects. In Melville's mind, they should have focused instead on work that would benefit all of humanity.

Melville stood outside in the January cold and watched the building burn.

Shortly after this episode, Melville developed a dangerous cough. A local doctor told him that the cough would probably kill him within two years. The news of his impending death only reinforced Melville's desire to make good use of his life. Melville knew that he would have to work harder and stay focused on his goals if he wanted to accomplish something before his death.

Although the cough improved, Melville never forgot that his time on Earth was limited. He focused on his desire to reform education. Melville believed that too much time was wasted in schools. In his day, most children were educated in one-room schoolhouses. One teacher taught students of every grade at the same time. Most students only attended school until they were proficient in reading and basic math. Very few went on to a secondary academy or college. Melville wanted to make a more efficient system that would allow students to learn more in less time.

In the spring of 1870, Melville enrolled in Alfred University, a Seventh Day Baptist school. But Melville was interested in a more prestigious education. He decided not to go back to Alfred for a second term. Instead, in October 1870, Melville enrolled in Amherst College, in Amherst, Massachusetts. It was here that Melville would take steps to reform libraries in the United States.

AT AMHERST COLLEGE IN 1874

AT COLUMBIA UNIVERSITY IN 1885

SECRETARY OF REGENTS, U. S. N. Y.
ALBANY, 1899

© UNDERWOOD & UNDERWOOD
AT LAKE PLACID CLUB, N. Y., 1922

Dewey's dedication to reform would stay with him throughout his life.

Delta Kappa Epsilon House at Amherst College

THE ASSISTANT LIBRARIAN

*D*ewey was determined to focus on his studies at Amherst College. He was serious about his education and his commitment to reform. Shortly before the beginning of the school term, Dewey wrote in his diary,

I shall mingle in society very little during the next four years. . . . I shall take the course which I think will give me the most thoro [sic] culture and the greatest ability to do good.[1]

Dewey's college plans did not include much time for recreation. Though he became a member of the Delta Kappa Epsilon fraternity, he made few lasting friendships. Dewey disliked smoking, drinking, and idle conversation. Most social activities of the time included at least one of these behaviors. So, Dewey proudly declined most social engagements, saying that he did not have time for such things. In his diary, Dewey wrote, "My social expenses are less than other boys because I keep clear of nearly all of them and am satisfied."[2]

At Amherst, first-year students learned Latin, Greek, algebra, geometry, and trigonometry. By graduation, students would have taken courses in the various sciences and in classical literature and philosophy. An education at Amherst exposed students to various "universal truths" but shied away from discussions of modern issues, such as abolition and other important topics to the reformers in Dewey's hometown. Politics and contemporary literature were discussed sparingly, if at all.

Dewey worked at the Amherst Library.

The Amherst Library

On October 20, 1872, during Dewey's junior year, he took a job as a student assistant at the Amherst Library. College was expensive for Dewey. The meager pay he received from his library job helped reduce some of his debt.

Few students used the library often. Amherst professors required their students to purchase textbooks for their classes. Readings and recitations were assigned directly from these books, making outside reading unnecessary.

But Dewey believed the library was a great resource. He saw in it a potential to educate the masses and decided to devote himself to this cause. Expanding the reach of the library fit well with his mission of education reform.

RESEARCH

Soon after starting work at the library, Dewey noted that the system used to shelve books was problematic. Each book was assigned a fixed location on the shelf, regardless of what other books surrounded it. Dewey decided that he needed to know more about libraries and their operations, and he began to read a wide range of literature on the subject. In January 1873, Dewey read Charles C. Jewett's "The Plan for Stereotyping Catalogues by Separate

"I always realized that out of a score of things that had greatly attracted me, I could do only one with one life and so I determined that my highest usefulness would be . . . to stimulate others to take up the work . . . seeking out and inspiring and guiding others to do the work for which my one life did not give time."[3]
—Melvil Dewey, explaining his decision to dedicate himself to reform

Main Classes of the Dewey Decimal Classification

The Dewey Decimal Classification has been updated over time. Following are its modern categories:

000–099: Computer science, knowledge, and general works
100–199: Philosophy and psychology
200–299: Religion
300–399: Social sciences, sociology, and anthropology
400–499: Language
500–599: Science and mathematics
600–699: Technology
700–799: Arts and recreation
800–899: Literature, rhetoric, and criticism
900–999: History, geography, and biography

Titles, and for Forming a General Stereotyped Catalogue of Public Libraries in the United States," which recommended building a universal catalog by which books could be arranged.

Later that year, Dewey visited libraries in New York and Boston, Massachusetts, to continue his research on classification systems. Dewey disliked Jacob Schwartz's system at the New York State Library, which arranged books alphabetically, without any consideration of their subject. However, he was impressed by the library's system of recording titles on index cards. In Boston, Dewey met with Charles A. Cutter. Dewey was impressed by Cutter, who classified books on horses under the subject of *horse* rather than *zoology*.

Dewey returned to Amherst and continued his research. William Torrey Harris, of St. Louis Public Schools, wrote an article recommending arrangement of books alphabetically under each subject. Dewey also read a pamphlet by Nathaniel Shurtleff, who proposed using a decimal system. The article intrigued Dewey, though he disliked many of the details of Shurtleff's system.

After all this research, Dewey had much to consider. He admired certain aspects of many of these systems, but their weaknesses were troubling. When Dewey finally created his decimal system, he had not truly invented a new system. Instead, he had found a way to combine the best parts of the systems by Jewett, Schwartz, Cutter, Harris, and Shurtleff.

On May 8, 1873, Dewey presented his proposal for a new classification to the Library Committee of Amherst. He continued to refine his system, even writing to William Harris for advice.

Dewey's Horse

One of the things that attracted Dewey to Amherst College was its requirement that students get regular exercise. Dewey's exercise consisted of only horseback riding. In the summer of 1874, Dewey bought his own horse. He rode it twice a day, six days a week.

ANOTHER YEAR AT AMHERST

On July 9, 1874, Dewey graduated from Amherst College, a major accomplishment at the time for a person of Dewey's background and financial means. After graduation, Dewey accepted a temporary position as assistant librarian at Amherst to implement his ideas. This gave Dewey time to work on his system. His initial proposal to the Library Committee had described how the books could be put in order but did not say what that order would be.

Finding a Home

In 1874, Dewey had a bit of trouble finding a place to live. He rented a room in a home near Amherst College. The home belonged to William Hunt. However, Hunt had recently arranged to swap houses with Mrs. S. G. Pratt, who wanted to move closer to her church and her children's school. Pratt asked Dewey to help her with her business dealings and offered him a room in her house. Dewey agreed to stay.

On March 29, 1874, Dewey helped both Hunt and the Pratt family with their respective moves. Shortly afterward, in going through Pratt's financial accounts, Dewey discovered that Hunt had unfairly made $1,500 on the exchange. Dewey confronted Hunt, who accused Dewey of meddling in other people's affairs. Unsure of how to proceed, Dewey dropped the matter.

Soon, others noticed the discrepancy. A local businessman suggested that, as Hunt and Pratt had moved prior to signing the official deeds to their houses, they return to their original houses. The two agreed to this suggestion, wanting to avoid a lawsuit. By April 29, Hunt and Pratt had moved back into their original homes. At the request of Mrs. Pratt, Dewey moved into her home.

While Dewey plugged away at his decimal system, he also worked to spread other reforms. Dewey taught a freshman class at Amherst on shorthand, a fast method of writing by using symbols. Initially, the administration refused to give students academic credit for the course. So, Dewey offered to teach the class for free if the students could receive credit. The administration gladly accepted his offer.

During this year, Dewey also dropped the "le" from the end of his first name, showing his dedication to spelling reform. Dewey argued that spelling reform prevented students from wasting time memorizing the peculiarities of the English language. He also believed that simplified spelling would allow immigrants to more easily learn English and assimilate into American culture.

Dewey was enjoying his work at the library, as well. He continued

Congregational Church

After graduation, Dewey joined a local Congregational church. Though the beliefs are similar, Congregationalists are more subdued than Evangelical Baptists. They seek reform, but they prefer to do so quietly, without drawing too much attention to themselves.

Dewey admitted that his choice to join the church was primarily for social reasons. A number of unmarried women attended the church. Dewey was seriously interested in one of these women for a time.

to refine his decimal system. Dewey wrote letters to many librarians interested in classification, and he sent them drafts of his work in progress. He also consulted with members of the Amherst faculty, asking their advice on the best subject headings for areas of study that he was not very familiar with. Dewey's hard work paid off, and by November 1875, he had completed his system. He was ready to have it published.

William Torrey Harris recommended arranging books
alphabetically by subject.

Dewey moved to the bustling city of Boston to work with Edwin Ginn in 1876.

THE YEAR OF THE LIBRARY

In December 1875, Dewey traveled to Boston on business for Amherst Library. He went to sell books that the library no longer needed. During his trip, Dewey met with Edwin Ginn, the owner of an educational publishing company. Ginn was interested in working with Dewey. Although Amherst was publishing initial copies of Dewey's decimal classification, Ginn wanted to publish future editions as well as materials on the metric system. Ginn also offered Dewey a job with his company. Excited by the prospect of working on educational reform in Boston, Dewey accepted Ginn's offer. On April 10, 1876, Dewey packed up his belongings and moved to Boston.

The Library Publication

In Boston, Dewey went straight to work on his metric system reform. In May, he traveled to New York for an American Metrological Society meeting. While in New York, Dewey visited the offices of *Publishers Weekly* and met with editors Frederick Leypoldt and Richard R. Bowker. Dewey wanted to publish a monthly journal about library

Perceptions of Dewey

William F. Poole was wary of giving his support for Dewey's library conference. He did not know Dewey, but he had heard that Dewey was "a tremendous talker and a little of an old maid."[1] He held off on giving his endorsement until Charles A. Cutter, director of the Boston Athenaeum, assured him that Dewey was "no imposter, humbug, speculator, dead beat, or anything of the sort."[2]

issues. Leypoldt, who had already
been considering publishing such
a journal, was very interested in
Dewey's idea.

Leypoldt hired Dewey as managing
editor in Boston of the new *American
Library Journal.* The publication would
cover a wide range of issues about
the library field. It would include
practical advice for librarians and
discussions on the role of libraries
in society. The first issue of the
American Library Journal was published
on September 30, 1876. Dewey's
article in the issue, "The Profession,"
stated,

> The time was when a library was very
> much like a museum, and a librarian was
> a mouser in musty books, and visitors
> looked with curious eyes at ancient tomes
> and manuscripts. The time is when a
> library is a school, and the librarian is in
> the highest sense a teacher, and the visitor
> is a reader among the books as a workman
> among his tools.[3]

Libraries in the United States

Many early libraries in the United States belonged to ministers. In the late seventeenth century, minister Thomas Bray established the first free library in the colonies. John Harvard, another clergyman, helped establish the oldest academic library in the United States. His library became the Harvard University Library. Subscription libraries, in which patrons paid dues to use the library, became popular in the eighteenth century. Not until the early 1850s, when free public education was becoming popular, were tax-supported public libraries established.

Dewey hoped that librarians would take pride in their profession and accept responsibility for educating the public.

Planning a Library Conference

At their first meeting, Leypoldt had told Dewey that he was planning to arrange a meeting of librarians in Philadelphia that year, on the nation's centennial, or hundredth anniversary. This would improve communication and cooperation among librarians.

Dewey loved the idea. He drafted letters asking several prominent librarians to

Fiction in Libraries

William F. Poole presented a paper on fiction in libraries at the first American Library Association (ALA) conference. The paper generated a heated discussion among the attendees. Poole believed that reading fiction did not lead to immoral or irresponsible behaviors.

However, many conference attendees disagreed with Poole. They said that reading fiction could influence a person's behavior. At the time, many professionals agreed that members of the public were not able to choose their own reading materials wisely. As such, it was the librarians' role to choose books for their collections that would benefit society. Dewey agreed with this idea. Choosing books to benefit society appealed to his sense of reform.

However, librarians faced difficulty determining what fiction was "good" or "bad." They could agree that the classics they had read in school were good. But what was bad fiction? And how could they identify it? The fiction debate was not resolved at the conference, but many remained firm in their opposition to holding so-called bad fiction in their collections.

Today, the ALA is opposed to the banning of books from libraries, calling the practice a form of censorship.

endorse the meeting as well. Many agreed to the meeting immediately. Two respected librarians, Justin Winsor of the Boston Public Library and William F. Poole of the Chicago Public Library, were wary of Dewey and did not give their support. However, Winsor's and Poole's support would be necessary to the conference's success. Through persistence and flattery, Dewey and Leypoldt were able to gain these men's support. Finally, with full endorsement, Dewey sent out a call for the conference on June 9, 1876.

"The people are more and more getting their incentives and ideas from the printed page. There are more readers and fewer listeners, and men who move and lead the world are using the press more and the platform less. It needs no argument to prove that reading matter can be distributed better and more cheaply through lending libraries than in any other way."[4]
—*Melvil Dewey*

THE FIRST CONFERENCE

The conference began on October 4, 1876, in Philadelphia, with 103 librarians in attendance. Though Dewey was not yet 25 years old and the youngest man at the meeting, he was a prominent figure.

At the conference, a permanent organization for librarians was

The ALA has held many conferences throughout the years.
The first conference began on October 4, 1876.

established, the American Library Association
(ALA). Dewey was the first to sign the register.
He suggested that the conference members elect a
board of officers to oversee the writing of the ALA's
constitution and by-laws. Dewey was elected secretary
and treasurer. The *American Library Journal* was also
adopted as the ALA's official journal.

THE AMHERST CLASSIFICATION

The last important development in librarianship
in 1876 was Dewey's classification system. The DDC
was published anonymously in 1876, though Dewey

is listed as the copyright holder.
Originally titled *A Classification and
Subject Index for Cataloguing and Arranging
the Books and Pamphlets of a Library*, it
was more often referred to as the
Amherst Classification. Originally,
Dewey had developed the system
for use at Amherst. The college had
copies printed for use in its library
and agreed to print additional copies
for Dewey's own use.

Many librarians were eager to
discuss Dewey's system at the ALA
conference. But Dewey was reluctant
to do so. He did not want others to
think he had organized the meeting
to promote his classification system.
He gave only a brief presentation on
his system.

He then allowed attendees to
fill out requests for copies of the
Special Report on Public Libraries, which
included a more detailed explanation
of the system. With this publication,
Dewey gained new fame for his work.

**First Board of Officers
for the American
Library Association**

- Justin Winsor, president
- William F. Poole, vice
  president
- A. R. Spofford, vice
  president
- Henry Homes, vice
  president
- Melvil Dewey, secre-
  tary and treasurer

Though Dewey had shared much of his system with other librarians in letters and conversations, only a few people had the privilege of knowing the full extent of the system.

Immediately, Dewey's classification was recognized as an important system, and many librarians were eager to use it in their own libraries. Even those who did not fully understand the system praised it. Charles A. Cutter, director of the Boston Athenaeum, wrote,

> *I cannot pretend yet to fully understand the [scheme] in all its details and in all its bearings, but so far as I do comprehend it, it seems to me [one] of the most important contributions to library economy that has been made for many years.* [5]

The year 1876 saw many advances in librarianship: the establishment of a monthly library publication, the founding of an organization for librarians, and the acceptance

Description of Dewey

William E. Foster, an attendee at the first ALA conference, described Dewey at that time:
"He is an extremely lithe, wiry, and 'lively' person. His mental activity is plainly as pronounced as his physical activity. . . . He appears almost smooth-shaven having a moustache only, in contrast to most of the others present. . . . Despite his youth, he is accustomed to wear spectacles to help his vision. His voice is rather high-pitched than otherwise." [6]

of Dewey's classification system. Dewey was greatly encouraged by these successes. He moved forward with confidence in his plans for other reforms.

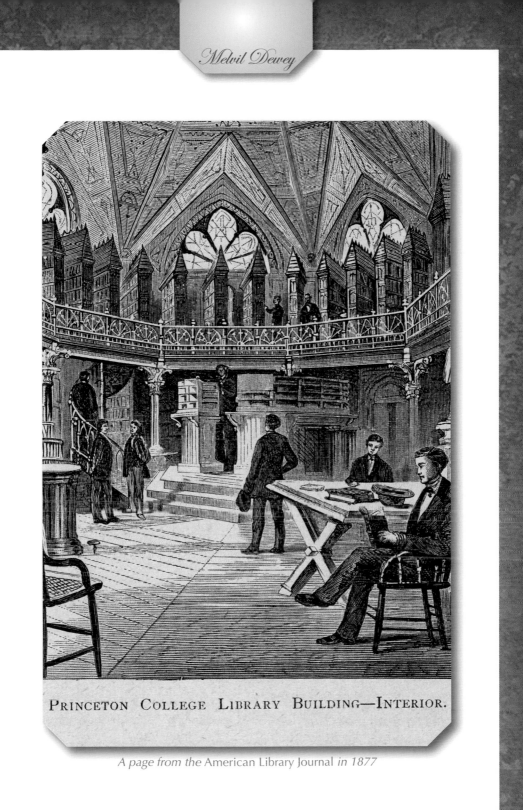

PRINCETON COLLEGE LIBRARY BUILDING—INTERIOR.

A page from the American Library Journal *in 1877*

Dewey endorsed the use of metric measurements in the United States.

MOVING FORWARD

Although much of his time was taken up by his classification system and other library work, Dewey was still able to make progress on some of his other reforms. He remained passionate about the need in the United States for simplified spelling and the implementation of the metric system.

The American Metric Bureau

With funds from Ginn and other investors, as well as a lot of his own money, Dewey began a metric organization. By July 4, 1876, Dewey had incorporated the American Metric Bureau (AMB). The bureau would sell rulers, thermometers, barometers, conversion charts, and other instructional devices.

Dewey assumed that as the American Metrical Society, of which he was a part, gained more influence, more institutions would adopt the metric system. This would ensure demand for AMB's products. On July 28, 1876, Dewey hosted the first AMB meeting. He served as the both secretary and treasurer, but according to his own written by-laws, he would not receive a salary for his work. In August, Dewey sent out the first issue of *Metric Bulletin*, the AMB's official publication.

Dewey solicited new members and encouraged colleges and universities to use the metric system. By 1877, the AMB had 140 members. Dewey was especially proud of his success with the U.S. Post

Office. He convinced them to adopt a standard-sized postcard measuring 7.5 by 12.5 centimeters (2.9 by 4.9 in). This was also the standard card size Dewey proposed be used in library card catalogs. Library card catalogs were an important system that helped people find books in the library before electronic card catalogs were possible. Index cards on every book in the library were filed in alphabetical order. People looking for a certain book would find the index card for the book. The index card would list the book's location in the library. Now, the size of card catalog cards and postcards were the same. Dewey had a habit of trying to merge elements of his various reforms. By doing so, Dewey hoped to make standard methods and sizes both natural and desirable.

SPELLING REFORM ASSOCIATION

Meanwhile, Dewey was also working on spelling reform. Radical spelling reformers supported an overhaul of English spelling. They proposed spelling words phonetically, or exactly as the words were pronounced. Others favored a gradual change. They favored such changes as dropping the silent *e* at the end of a word or substituting an *f* for *ph*. Dewey was among the gradual reformers, though he was one of the most enthusiastic. As with his other reforms, he proposed starting a monthly journal and creating a bureau to supply teaching devices and other supplies.

In August 1876, Dewey attended a conference on spelling reform in Philadelphia, which resulted in the formation of the Spelling Reform Association (SRA). Dewey was elected its secretary and later became treasurer. By October, the members agreed to write to newspaper, magazine, and book editors and persuade them to adopt simplified spelling.

A PERFECT MATCH

Dewey also lectured on his Amherst Classification. In 1876, he presented the system to a group of librarians and assistants at Harvard University in Cambridge, Massachusetts. Annie Roberts Godfrey, a young librarian of Wellesley College, was in attendance.

At first, Dewey and Godfrey's relationship was purely professional.

Daily Regimen

To make good use of time, Annie and Melvil Dewey developed their own daily schedules. At the beginning of every month, they would make resolutions for personal improvement. An example of Annie's list read, "Exercise 1 hr; Self-Culture, 1 hr; Sing 15 min; Don't waste a minute." Dewey's read, "Horse-back 3 a week; Dress well; Short, organized letters; Rise early, eat slowly; Make no promises; Breathe deeply, sing, and settle cash daily."[1] At the end of the month, the couple would evaluate their progress and change their lists as needed.

Dewey and Godfrey met at a conference at Harvard University in Cambridge, Massachusetts.

They exchanged letters about their common library problems. Godfrey was one of only ten women in attendance at the first ALA conference in Philadelphia. In 1877, she and Dewey were part of a small group of librarians who traveled to England for the Conference of Librarians held in London. The Library Association of the United Kingdom was also established at that meeting.

During the trip, Godfrey and Dewey became better acquainted. Godfrey noted in her letters home that Dewey made one of the best speeches at the meeting. She also observed that Dewey's eagerness to create change often meant that he took on more work than his colleagues. Like Dewey, Godfrey was serious, hardworking, and reform minded. But she was reluctant to move beyond friendship with Dewey because of her great respect for his work. She was unsure if her presence in his life would help him or hold him back.

In the end, her attraction for Dewey won out. The two married at Milford, Massachusetts, on October 19, 1878. During their marriage, Annie Dewey always put her husband's work first. She supported all of his attempts at reform. She sympathized with him and offered him advice. Dewey had little money when they married, and Annie constantly reminded him of the restraints of time and money in completing his work. She also watched his health. If not for her reproaches, Dewey would often have worked late into the night and eaten too quickly.

An Unselfish Life

Annie Dewey thought that her husband's devotion to reform was admirable, but she worried that he took on too much responsibility. On his birthday, December 10, 1877, she wrote him a letter that read: "I am glad that another year is added to your unselfish life; glad that it is a power for good; glad that you are my friend, that I may be yours. . . . Your crowded busy life is one to be envied in comparison to mine, only you are doing very wrong to put on more steam than any human machine is warranted to run under."[2]

A LIBRARY SUPPLY COMPANY

Dewey pushed the ALA to develop the Supply Department, which would supply educational material and specialized equipment to libraries. But the ALA was slow in expanding the department to meet Dewey's expectations. He eventually pulled the Supply Department from the ALA. With the help of investors, he developed the Readers and Writers Economy Company (RWEC) in March 1879.

The Readers and Writers Economy Company

In 1879, Dewey formed the Readers and Writers Economy Company (RWEC). Under the RWEC, Dewey merged the interests of ALA, AMB, SRA, and the *Library Journal,* which had changed its name from *American Library Journal* in 1877. He combined all their accounts.

The RWEC sold specialized furniture and office supplies made for libraries. The RWEC was successful, but financial matters became difficult to keep straight. Dewey did not know how much he was due to be paid as the company's president. In 1880, he resigned as treasurer and a Committee on Past Salary was appointed to clarify the confusion in Dewey's books. By September, the committee had reviewed Dewey's accounts. But his combined accounts made it unclear who owned what.

In October 1880, the committee obtained a court order to prevent Dewey from doing his job so that they could audit, or review, the RWEC books. Insulted, Dewey immediately resigned. Unfortunately, some of Dewey's personal funds were tied up in RWEC accounts that he could no longer access. He was unable to pay debts and keep the ALA, AMB, and SRA afloat. On January 10, 1881, the matter was settled. Dewey's personal property and the property of the ALA, AMB, and SRA was returned to him. But Dewey did not receive compensation for any of his work with the RWEC.

Under RWEC, Dewey combined the accounts of the ALA, AMB, SRA, and *Library Journal,* which had changed its name from *American Library Journal* in 1877. By doing this, Dewey was able to draw from a larger pool of money for his various reforms. He believed that anyone who might scrutinize his unconventional business practices would recognize that they were not for his personal gain. He thought that the causes were so deserving of funding that no one would question his methods.

But Dewey did not always inform members of these associations or their investors of his financial methods. Eventually, Dewey's unusual financial methods were discovered. The RWEC accounts were jumbled and confusing. It was difficult to tell what money belonged to which organization. Dewey's relationship with RWEC was ended. Additionally, he was forced to resign from many of the treasury, secretary, and editor positions he held with other organizations.

During this turbulent period, Dewey also changed the spelling of his last name. On December 10, 1879, his twenty-eighth birthday, he officially became *Melvil Dui.* The move was another sign of his dedication to spelling reform.

Library Supplies

The Library Bureau supplied items that specifically met the needs of librarians. Such items included catalog cards and catalog cabinets for card catalog systems. Other items included book trucks, magazine racks, newspaper racks, map cases, and date stamps.

Though Dui had been pushed out of the RWEC, many people still believed him to be honest, well meaning, and an asset to their organizations. But Dui decided to keep a lower profile and focus on a new business. In March 1881, he opened the Library Bureau, which sold office supplies specially designed to meet the needs of libraries.

On May 31, Dui had the Library and Metric Bureaus incorporated, which means they became legal corporations. With an inheritance that Annie had received upon her father's death, the Duis were the majority shareholders in the new company. By now, Dui felt ready to move on to new challenges.

The RWEC sold library supplies such as catalog cards and catalog cabinets.

Columbia College in 1897

A Library School

lthough Dui's time in Boston was marked by many successes, it was also a period of financial chaos and frustration for him. So, in March 1883, when Columbia College president Frederick Augustus Porter Barnard wrote to Dui about an opening for a librarian-in-chief, Dui was eager to move to New York City and get the job. Several prominent librarians, including Poole and Cutter, recommended Dui for the position.

Dui visited the college in April. The Library Committee at Columbia College had allocated a $3,500 salary for its new librarian-in-chief. At the time, faculty members earned a standard salary of $5,000. Dui requested that he be paid the same as faculty. He also expressed interest in creating a school for librarians.

While visiting the college, Dui heard that some of his colleagues had criticized his eccentricities, such as the spelling of his name. Dui must have been concerned, because by April 18, he had changed his name back to Dewey. Poole, for one, was glad to see the change. On April 23, he wrote to Dewey, "I am very glad to see that you write your name Dewey.

Spelling at Columbia College

Dewey's colleagues at Columbia College were not sympathetic to his commitment to spelling reform. While at Columbia, Dewey was careful to use conventional spelling on any official documents or letters. He continued to use simplified spelling in his personal letters.

Now pray lay aside some, at least, of your [spelling] peculiarities, and spell like common folk."[1]

On May 7, 1883, Dewey was hired as librarian-in-chief of Columbia College in New York. His salary request had been turned down, but he accepted a rate of $3,500 a year.

LIBRARIAN-IN-CHIEF

The library at Columbia needed an overhaul, and Dewey seemed like just the man to do it. The new librarian would be responsible for reorganizing the library and consolidating the library's many collections into a single collection. The Library Committee also wanted the library to extend its hours and improve its acquisition of new books. The committee granted Dewey a sum of $10,000 to be used to institute these changes.

Dewey approached this challenge with his typical enthusiasm. He proposed increasing the library's operating hours from 15 hours per week to 14 hours per day. To accomplish this, Dewey would need to hire additional staff. Their support would be needed in consolidating the library collection, as well. Dewey notably hired seven women as librarians on the all-male campus. Dewey believed these college-educated

Dewey believed that women would make good librarians.

women had the right character for library work. He also knew that they would be willing to accept the jobs for less pay than their male counterparts.

In order to address the acquisition problems, Dewey asked faculty members for their suggestions on what books were needed and what books could be removed. Dewey wanted to buy only the best, most necessary books. He would rely on alumni gifts to round out other areas of the collection.

Rules of the Library

One of Dewey's concerns in the Columbia College Library was noise. He had rubber tips placed on tables and chairs and rubber wheels on book trucks. New library patrons were handed cards warning them against speaking, even whispering, when they were not near the loan desk. They were also told to step lightly when walking in the library.

Other rules included no tobacco use, no hats, and no putting feet on chairs or tables. Dewey thought these rules were so well advised that he had the Library Bureau print them and distribute them to other libraries.

Also, Dewey recognized that other libraries in the area already had some of the titles that Columbia's library was lacking. Dewey met with 72 New York City librarians on June 18, 1885, to discuss a way to share their collections through interlibrary loans. The New York Library Club was formed at this meeting. The group would work together to promote the interests of New York City libraries.

Despite some of his money-saving ideas, the Columbia College trustees were unhappy with the cost of Dewey's library. The reclassifying and reorganizing of the collection was a long process, and the trustees saw no end to it in sight. To cut costs, Dewey fired one of the library's longtime employees, William Baker. However, some of the faculty members were upset by this decision, and Dewey was forced to rehire Baker.

The School of Library Economy

Dewey had proposed starting a library school when he was hired. Columbia's trustees agreed to consider the idea, though they were not enthusiastic. Dewey was undeterred. College President Barnard presented Dewey's plans for the school on May 5, 1884. It was approved so long as it did not create debt for the university. Officials hoped the school would provide a good source of income for the college. In addition to his duties as librarian-in-chief, Dewey was given the title of professor of library economy.

Dewey advertised for applicants to the library school. However, he did so without permission from the trustees. He also encouraged women to apply. This upset some of the trustees and faculty. They did not think admitting women was appropriate, but they could not

Dewey's Other Interests

At Columbia, Dewey focused mainly on his work at the library and building his library school. Though he remained a member of the AMB and SRA, neither organization saw much success. The Library Bureau, on the other hand, did well during this period.

Dewey also remained a prominent member of the ALA. He attended conferences and revised his decimal classification in 1885.

ban Dewey from opening his school just because it included women. However, they could ban him from using Columbia's classrooms.

Unwilling to delay the opening of the school, Dewey found a way around the trustees' actions. He had a janitor set up an unused off-campus storeroom with classroom furniture. On January 5, 1887, the School of Library Economy opened on time. Twenty students had been accepted, 17 of whom were women.

Unfortunately, Dewey had underestimated the

Women in Librarianship

Dewey is sometimes praised for his work in encouraging women to become librarians. Education and librarianship are fields that today are dominated by women, but that was not always the case. In the late nineteenth century, professions that required a college education, such as those of librarians, were often dominated by men.

Dewey hired women to work under him at Columbia and admitted women to his library school against the wishes of the school's trustees. Both actions won him enemies during his tenure at the college. Although President Barnard favored admitting women to Columbia, a majority of the faculty and trustees opposed the practice.

As Martha T. Buckham, one of the librarians Dewey hired at Columbia, remembered, "Columbia College was almost hermetically sealed to women as in a monastery, . . . a group of young college women, appearing in the sacred precincts, must indeed have given occasion for dire forebodings."[2]

Dewey believed librarianship was a field most suited to women. Still, he relied heavily on the advice of the all-male faculty in acquiring new reading materials, which limited the librarians' roles. He also acknowledged that women could be paid less than men.

cost and the amount of time needed for his project. He could not hire a faculty for the library school. Instead, his staff and guest lecturers, who taught for free, ran the classes. Faculty from Columbia also lectured on reading material in their subject areas.

The Deweys lived in a small, seventh-floor apartment for most of their time in New York. Many of the guest speakers stayed at the Deweys' apartment when in town for lectures at the School of Library Economy. The Deweys also hosted gatherings with the library school students and staff every other week. They tried to cultivate a sense of family among the staff and students.

Opposition

Dewey ran his school under intense opposition from the trustees and most of the faculty members. Dewey often acted without permission from the trustees, believing that he would be proven right in the end. He printed pamphlets and reports on library matters, which he distributed to the faculty members. Most of them thought the literature was annoying and boastful. In addition, many people remained upset by Dewey's admitting women to the school and disliked him personally.

When President Barnard left Columbia College in 1888, Dewey faced greater opposition.

Although Dewey was aware of this opposition, he made no effort to appease his critics. His main focus was on keeping the library school open. Dewey needed more money to pay his staff, but he was refused. So, he funded the school with money originally designated for the reclassification of the library, which was coming to an end.

In May 1888, President Barnard resigned from his position at Columbia. Barnard had been a strong supporter of Dewey. Once he was gone, the trustees acted to remove Dewey from the college. Dewey was suspended from his position as chief librarian, and a special committee was formed to investigate his actions at Columbia.

Seth Low was a member of this committee. As the investigation began, Dewey told Low that he had been offered a position with the Regents of the University of the State of New York. The University of the State of New York was not an actual university. It was a governing body appointed to oversee higher education in the state of New York. It made sure that degrees were valid and credentialed professionals met certain basic standards. It also ran a program that allowed students to obtain degrees by passing certain

President Barnard

Frederick Augustus Porter Barnard was president of Columbia College from 1864 to 1889. Barnard worked to open Columbia to women. During his tenure, Columbia's enrollment increased, new departments were established, and the library was consolidated and improved.

On April 27, 1889, Barnard died. Barnard College for women, a school affiliated with Columbia, opened just six months after his death.

courses. The regents helped govern the University of the State of New York. Low was sympathetic to Dewey and understood that Dewey meant to accept the position with the regents. As a favor, Low limited his investigation to specific points regarding Dewey's conduct so as not to tarnish Dewey's reputation and prevent him from getting the position. So, on December 3, when Low submitted his report, he recommended that Dewey not be dismissed. A little over two weeks later, on December 20, 1888, Dewey resigned. —

Seth Low

The Deweys moved to Albany, New York, in 1888.

THE ALBANY YEARS

ewey accepted a position as regents'
secretary of the University of the State
of New York and as director of the New York
State Library in Albany. He would be responsible
for reorganizing the New York State Library and

improving the university's examinations. Each
of these positions was a full-time job in and of
itself. It was a huge undertaking, but Dewey was
characteristically eager to meet the challenge.

The Dewey family now included a son. Godfrey
Dewey had been born on September 3, 1887. In
mid-December 1888, the new family of three packed
up their belongings and moved upstate. Dewey began
work on January 1, 1889.

Dewey and Annie settled into life
in Albany. In 1890, they bought a
large, three-story home. It included
a library, parlor, dining room,
pantry, kitchen, billiard room, and
numerous bedrooms. The many
bedrooms allowed the Deweys to host
guests visiting the university. He also
rented out rooms to female state
library employees.

In addition, Annie's mother
moved in with the Deweys shortly
after they bought the house.
Eventually, the Deweys took in
other boarders for a rate of $35 a
month. The Deweys were known as

ALA Baby

Dewey was at a confer-
ence when Annie gave
birth to their son, Godfrey.
The conference attend-
ees took special note of
the occasion. They nick-
named Godfrey Dewey
the "ALA baby."

good entertainers and welcomed visitors to their home. The house was always filled with visitors—they had approximately 600 dinner guests a year.

THE REGENTS' SECRETARY

As regents' secretary, Dewey was in a position of some authority with the university. He was glad to be part of an organization that agreed "public libraries should be recognized as an essential part of the State system of higher education."[1] With the passage of a law Dewey wrote, he was able to increase the regents' power. The university's powers were extended. The New York State Library became an important part of the university, too. In addition, the regents were responsible for administering exams to teachers, medical students, and other professionals.

Dewey was especially concerned about the condition of education in

Impression of Dewey

Many people who came in contact with Dewey were impressed by him. Georgia Benedict encountered Dewey at the Albany State Library. She remembered: "I was ushered into an office where a black-haired, black-bearded, black-eyed gentleman . . . was working away with a kind of furious quiet at a big desk. I was struck by the speed and accuracy of his movements. It was like watching a fine machine. . . . the air around him was vibrant with his energy. His decisiveness, the sparkling darkness of his face . . . [and] his intense energy impressed me deeply."[2]

Dewey became director of the New York State Library in Albany.

New York. He wanted to make sure that all schools met certain standards. Some of them, often referred to as "diploma mills," awarded diplomas to all students who paid their tuition, regardless of how much they had learned. In 1891, Dewey helped pass a bill that required anyone who planned to practice medicine in New York to pass Regents Exams in medicine. This would help ensure that doctors were well educated.

By extending the power of the university and requiring certain examinations, Dewey was taking the first steps toward another goal. He believed the university should grant degrees to individuals who passed qualifying exams, even if they did not attend a school. Dewey believed that if individuals had studied a subject well enough on their own, they should be able to get degrees in their fields of expertise. He did not believe that such students should have to complete several years at the university if they had already mastered the subject matter of the courses. However, when

Office Efficiency

Dewey sought to bring efficiency to his offices in Albany. He recognized new inventions, such as the telephone and the typewriter, for their time-saving potential and encouraged their use in his offices.

In Dewey's office as regents' secretary, he instituted a secretarial pool. By sharing responsibilities, a secretary with time could help another who was busy. In this way, no one sat idle. By running the office more efficiently, Dewey was able to cut the number of employees from 27 to 13 in 1890. If the office was busy, he would hire temporary help to assist the regular staff.

As state librarian, Dewey designed his own desk. He created a bank of cubbyholes in which he put color-coded notes to his staff. The notes were written in shorthand, and they consisted of instructions, assignments, or communications from Dewey. The staff was expected to check their cubbyholes regularly. This system allowed Dewey to dispense instructions to his staff with minimal effort and without even having to look up from his desk.

Dewey proposed this idea in 1892, the regents unanimously opposed it.

Despite the opposition, Dewey continued to push for university extension so much that he was seen as a threat to the Department of Public Instruction. Under Dewey's supervision, a revised law had granted the regents more power in state education. Department members believed Dewey was trying to take control of secondary education in New York.

In response, Dewey changed his mission from "university extension" to "education extension." In other words, he was not greatly interested in controlling New York's schools; his real goal was to increase individual learning any way he could. His main focus with education extension was on home education. He wanted individuals to achieve through a combined effort of home study and instructor lectures.

THE STATE LIBRARIAN

In addition to his work as regents' secretary, Dewey was also director of the New York State Library. His first action as director was to move the library out of its temporary housing in the capitol building and into its own building. Dewey also took

**The New York
Library Association**

The New York Library Association (NYLA) was created in the summer of 1890, and Dewey served as its first president. The organization was intended to strengthen the role of libraries in society.

According to Dewey's vision, the NYLA would work on many fronts. It would push for the passage of laws that aided library work. In addition, the NYLA served as a professional organization for New York librarians. They could share ideas, books, and work together in other ways.

As state librarian, Dewey already had the authority to institute many of his plans for extending library services. But with the backing of an organization such as the NYLA, he would have even more power to push for reforms and funding from indifferent lawmakers.

on the responsibility of reclassifying the collection. He hired an old colleague, Walter Biscoe, for the job.

On January 10, 1889, Dewey proposed the transfer of Columbia College's Library School to Albany. The regents agreed to his proposal. By March 30, the transfer was complete, and the school became known as the New York State Library School. The school was similar to Columbia's program, but the regents were willing to grant degrees in Library Science to graduates.

In 1890, Dewey organized the New York Library Association (NYLA). He planned for public libraries to aid education in New York someday. When his plans for education came together, he wanted New York libraries to be ready for the task. Organized and efficient libraries were a key component in Dewey's education plans as regents' secretary.

Dewey extended the range of interlibrary loans. He also created a variety of programs and divisions for various library patrons. Dewey's creations included a medical division, a sociology division, a library for the blind, a woman's library, a capitol library, and a children's library. He also began a program in which traveling libraries brought books to rural areas that did not have libraries of their own. By the mid-1890s, the State Library's collection reached 500,000 volumes. Dewey also increased the library's collection of media other than books, including photographs, slides, and sheet music.

Many of Dewey's colleagues praised his work at the State Library, and they encouraged him to devote himself solely to that endeavor. His work as regents' secretary had been successful, as well. But he drew more criticism and had made more enemies in that role. Dewey ignored

Traveling Libraries

Five members of Dewey's staff at the State Library were on the "book board." These members chose 1,000 books from the State Library's collection that they thought were the most informative and best recreational reading. From this collection, 100 books (no more than 25 of them fiction) were boxed and sent to smaller public libraries for six-month loan periods. These traveling collections helped bring the best reading to small communities.

both suggestions and complaints and forged ahead in his plans for the university. ⌒

During his time in Albany, Dewey received both criticism and praise.

The ALA participated in the 1893 Chicago World's Fair.

RISE AND FALL

While working in Albany, Dewey continued to have an important impact on library issues on the national level. In 1890, he was elected the president of the ALA. However, only a few months later, he resigned due to health problems. Lucky for Dewey, he was elected again in 1892. Dewey's term as president was brief, but it was anything but dull.

Work with the ALA

Almost immediately after Dewey's second election, his power was challenged by Poole and his supporters. They requested that Mary S. Cutler, a Dewey supporter, step down from her position on a committee. They said that Cutler could not be as effective as a man. Their request was denied. Dewey's term as ALA president was characterized by similar power struggles.

As president, Dewey helped plan the ALA's participation in the 1893 Chicago World's Fair. The World's Fair was an exposition that displayed exhibits of new inventions, cultures, and arts from around the world. The ALA presented its exhibit of a "Model

World's Fair

A world's fair is an international exposition. Both government organizations and private companies may display their latest developments for the entertainment of the public. Exhibits may relate to commerce, industry, and science or showcase culture and art. But world's fairs are known best for featuring the latest inventions and scientific discoveries. Some products that have been shown at world's fairs include the Colt revolver, the telephone, the automobile, and the television.

Library," which would include 5,000 "best books." These titles were listed in the *ALA Catalog*, a publication Dewey had been pushing for during the past 16 years.

Dewey's successes were sometimes accomplished by manipulating other members of ALA. For example, despite opposition, Dewey managed to publish the *ALA Catalog* in decimal order. But Dewey's actions were noticed by many ALA members, and they grew suspicious of Dewey and his motives. Many worried that rather than working to benefit the ALA, Dewey was always searching for the best way to promote himself, no matter the costs.

RESIGNATION

At the university, too, Dewey's colleagues were growing suspicious and hostile toward him. But Dewey easily disregarded these feelings. His motivations were always to further

Maintaining the ALA

Even before Dewey was elected president of the ALA, his rivals began to plan a separate international congress of librarians. Originally, the congress was supposed to meet after the ALA conference meetings, so that everyone who was interested could attend. But after Dewey became ALA president, they wanted to meet separately from the ALA. This action challenged the authority of the ALA. Dewey managed to ensure that the conferences were not separate, securing the ALA's place. Later, Dewey created forums for special interest groups, which might have otherwise broken away from the ALA.

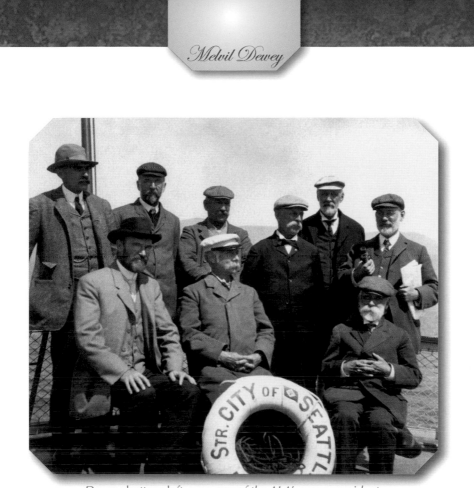

Dewey, bottom left, was one of the ALA's many presidents throughout the years.

his causes. In 1898, Governor Theodore Roosevelt praised the State Library and Dewey's work there in his inaugural address. Roosevelt also served as chairman of the library committee in 1899. He appointed a committee to plan for the unification of the state's educational departments. The unification plan renewed hostilities between the regents and the Department of Public Instruction.

On December 22, 1899, the regents held a meeting to discuss educational unification. Their authority was in jeopardy. Dewey, seeing that his position contributed to the conflict, resigned as secretary.

Dewey's resignation was regretfully accepted. With Dewey's position empty, the reorganization would move more smoothly. But the regents regarded Dewey as an asset to their organization, and they were sad to lose him. Dewey's successor, James Russell Parsons, remarked that under Dewey's tenure as regents' secretary, "the University came to be recognized as one of the most effective educational organizations in the United States."[1]

In 1904, the Unification Act was passed. It combined the university and the Department of Public Instruction. The resulting organization was the State Department of Education.

Regretful Resignation

The board accepted Dewey's resignation as regents' secretary with deep regret, saying, "The board recognize in Mr. Dewey an organizer of genius, an executive of great skill, an educational leader of marked originality and energy, and an officer whose administration has coincided with the largely augmented usefulness and honor of the University."[2]

Dewey was named Director of Libraries and Home Education. He reported to Andrew Sloan Draper, the Commissioner of Education. Draper quickly let Dewey know that he did not approve of Dewey's projects, and he openly questioned their usefulness.

LAKE PLACID CLUB

Dewey devoted himself more fully to his work at the State Library, the Library School, and the Department of Libraries and Home Education. He also focused more of his attention on a side

The Lake Placid Club

For a long time, Annie and Melvil Dewey had planned to buy a summer home and create a community around it. They believed that being close to nature was important. They also recognized the health benefits of the fresh air, which helped them find relief from their summer allergies.

During the summer, the Deweys often traveled to various locations to scout a good place to build such a community. In 1890, they visited Lake Placid, which was not too far from Albany. And, in 1892, the nearby Adirondack Park was created. In 1893, the Deweys purchased a 70-acre (28-ha) plot of land on Mirror Lake in Lake Placid. Shortly after, they also bought an adjacent plot of land with a large house on it.

The Deweys invited a select group of friends to stay with them on the property. They wanted to create a retreat for middle-class families. They hoped to cultivate a social community designed to give hardworking members of social professions an opportunity to rest and rejuvenate. The Deweys continued to purchase adjacent properties and make improvements, such as adding a tennis court and a golf course. Dewey wrote letters urging people to become members of the Lake Placid Club. The club soon became a success. It was a well-known and popular destination for family retreats.

project that he and Annie had been working on—the Lake Placid Club. The Deweys had purchased land on Lake Placid in the Adirondacks. They would vacation there to escape the ragweed and pollen that aggravated their allergies. In 1894, Dewey remodeled a boarding house on the property. He invited guests to the clubhouse the following year and formed the Lake Placid Club, a summer recreation spot.

CONTROVERSY

From the beginning, Dewey had been selective about the members he invited to the club. But by 1905, the club had become popular, and his selectiveness was called into serious question. The regents received a petition calling for Dewey's dismissal as state librarian because of his refusal to admit Jewish people to the club. Eleven prominent Jewish citizens signed the petition. Many of

Ethnic Objection

Henry Leipziger attended the annual New York Library Association's Library Week at the Lake Placid Club in 1903. Though Leipziger had tried, he had not been able to get a membership to the popular club on his own. While in the lobby, Leipziger read the club catalog, which said that Jewish people were not permitted to stay as guests at the club. Outraged, Leipziger returned to New York City and approached a Jewish lawyer with his complaint. They believed that because Dewey held a public office, his exclusion of Jewish people from the club gave other businesses the idea that they could discriminate as well. A petition was promptly drafted to remove Dewey from his position at the State Library.

Dewey's fellow librarians came to his defense, as well as some prominent Jewish citizens. But the question of Dewey's discrimination against Jewish people had been widely publicized. The regents could not ignore the situation. Draper issued a public reproach of Dewey.

Dewey claimed that the facts had been misrepresented. But on September 30, 1905, he offered his resignation, and it was accepted. Many librarians across the country were saddened by Dewey's resignation. He had been a formidable presence in their profession. The New York Library Association issued a statement upon Dewey's resignation, saying, "To him possibly more than any one person is due the present day intelligent appreciation of the place and value of the public library."[3]

Unfortunately, more problems lay ahead for Dewey. In 1906, several ALA women claimed that Dewey had acted inappropriately toward them during a trip following the ALA conference in 1905. Speculation had begun in the 1880s that Dewey had sexually harassed many other women. But this was the first time any women spoke out against Dewey's behavior. Dewey denied the accusations and claimed the women were unfairly slandering him. Still, the controversy marked the end of Dewey's leadership within the ALA. Dewey would have to find a new project to occupy his time.

The Lake Placid Club

Dewey, lower left, posed with the ex-presidents of the ALA in 1918.

THE LAST YEARS

Immediately after resigning at the State Library, Dewey focused all his energy on the Lake Placid Club. In May 1906, he moved there permanently. He and Annie were determined to make the club a success.

The club successfully operated as a summer resort. In 1906, Dewey began making plans to open the resort to winter vacationers, as well. Sports such as sledding, skiing, and skating were added to the activities. The Deweys wanted the club to set a model for healthy living and so banned liquor, tobacco, and gambling. Although Dewey faced many financial troubles with the club, it continued to appear successful. In 1895, the club had five acres (2 ha), one building, and $5,000 annual income. By 1905, it had 6,000 acres (2,428 ha), 225 buildings, and $500,000 annual income.

LIFE AT THE CLUB

Dewey continued to share close relationships with some of his fellow librarians. May Saymour and Katharine L. Sharp were trusted allies who helped the Dewey family

Fiftieth Anniversary

Although Dewey had taken a less active role in the ALA, he was asked to speak at the fiftieth anniversary conference in Atlantic City, New Jersey. Dewey's speech was titled "Our Next Half Century." The speech was well received. Those in attendance understood that library reform was still a dear concern to Dewey.

Annie and Melvil Dewey in 1918

with the club. When Sharp died in 1914, Emily Beal was invited to join the club's administrative staff and take over Sharp's duties. Beal also took over many of Annie's duties when her health began to fail in 1916.

Annie's health worsened. She went blind and had to learn to read and type by touch. Although she had been feeling stronger during the summer of 1922, Annie died on August 25, 1922. Dewey lost both his wife and his strongest ally. Annie had always supported Dewey's causes above her own. While at the Lake Placid Club, they had begun to take on a variety of new causes, such as cremation, eugenics, birth control, prohibition, women's suffrage, and the League of Nations.

But even with the loss of his most trusted partner, Dewey's plans for the club moved forward. Earlier that year, Dewey had formed the Lake Placid Club Education Foundation. Its goals were to restore efficiency to education, to help students achieve their full potential, and to promote other educational campaigns. Through the foundation, Dewey continued to promote metric conversion and simplified spelling.

LAKE PLACID CLUB SOUTH

After Annie's death, Dewey began to spend more time with Emily Beal. Beal had been a good friend to Annie during the end of her life, and Dewey came to rely on her. On May 28, 1924, Dewey and Emily married at the Lake Placid Club Chapel.

In 1925, Dewey caught the flu and became severely ill. His doctors recommended that he travel to a warmer climate to recuperate. Dewey and Emily began to travel more regularly to Florida, where they decided to found another club. With Emily's help, Dewey decided on a location in Lake Sterns, Florida. In 1927, he established the Lake Placid Club South. Florida lawmakers agreed to Dewey's request to change the name of the town from Lake Stearns to Lake Placid.

The Lake Placid Club in New York was doing well, but some members disapproved of the southern branch. Some of the club's trustees thought Dewey was being foolish to start a new venture so late in his life. Dewey was in his seventies and in poor health. They also worried that Dewey would use funds from Lake Placid North to support the new resort if it faltered.

Dewey was confident that Lake Placid South would be just as successful as the original venture. He took pleasure in recounting the success of Lake Placid North to local residents. Dewey hoped to develop Lake Placid South with the cooperation of the town. The community caught Dewey's enthusiasm for the project and began to take steps to make the town more inviting to tourists. They planted flowers on Main Street and built a fountain in the town square.

But the economy in Florida was not booming, and Dewey lacked money to fund the project. He pushed forward regardless and immediately ran into trouble. He was unable to make necessary improvements to the club in time for the opening.

The Deweys took out as many loans as they could. They also asked for support from Lake Placid North. But many members there were not in favor of the Florida venture. Godfrey Dewey, who was running Lake Placid North, acted in the best interest of the club and denied his father the money. Dewey was angry with his son. He believed that Godfrey had been turned against him. In the end, Dewey accepted the club's decision and offered his son a half-hearted apology.

Dewey traveled back and forth between New York and Florida. When the Great Depression hit in the early 1930s, both the North and South clubs felt the effects. Lake Placid South was failing, and Lake Placid North was barely staying afloat. Dewey stayed in Florida, determined to do everything he could to keep Lake Placid South going.

Saying Good-bye

On his eightieth birthday, Dewey was staying at Lake Placid South. He wrote a letter to some of his close friends. In the letter, he recounted some of his life's successes and spoke of his life at the club. He wrote in simplified spelling, a cause that his son, Godfrey, had taken up. But he warned his readers, "Melvil Dewey is not a watch that wears out to be discarded but lyk a sun dial wher no wheels get rusti or slip a cog or get tired [and] long for rest."[1]

But Dewey's health was failing. He died a little more than two weeks later on December 26, 1931. A funeral was held a few days later in Lake Placid, Florida, and a memorial service was held at Lake Placid North. Nearly 400 friends, family members, and employees attended the service. Dewey's ashes were later

Power Struggle

After Dewey's death, the question arose of who would carry on his work. Emily and Godfrey Dewey both wanted to become president of the Lake Placid Education Foundation. The board of trustees met on January 24, 1932, to discuss the vacancy.

Godfrey Dewey was a member of the board, but as a candidate for the presidency, he was not present at the vote. One of the trustees voted in Godfrey's favor, and the other 12 voted against him. Emily Dewey's candidacy was not given consideration at all. Arthur Bestor, one of the other trustees, was elected president to complete Dewey's term.

Also at the meeting, Emily proposed that a biography of Dewey be published on December 10, 1932, what would have been his eighty-first birthday. She projected the cost at $3,000. Emily probably wanted the biography published as a way to bring some focus back to Lake Placid South. The project was approved, and an author was commissioned. George Grosvenor Dawe's *Melvil Dewey, Seer: Inspirer: Doer* met the 1932 deadline.

placed in a family vault in the North Elba Cemetery near Lake Placid Club North.

Without Dewey's unwavering enthusiasm and leadership, the Lake Placid Club floundered. Many of the strict rules Dewey had instituted were abandoned in order to attract new visitors. Lake Placid South, despite Emily's best efforts, did not survive the Great Depression. The club grounds were sold in 1946.

DEWEY'S LEGACY

To accomplish many of his goals, Dewey often pushed boundaries. Though he had a group of steady supporters, many of his colleagues disliked him. In addition, Dewey often falsely believed that the end results of his reform efforts would justify any shortcuts he took to achieve them. Dewey lost the Readers and Writers Economy Company and had trouble with some other projects because of this kind of shortsightedness. Despite some of Dewey's shortcomings, his leadership

The Olympic Games

In 1932, the year after Dewey's death, the Winter Olympics were held at Lake Placid. Dewey's son Godfrey organized the event. The Lake Placid Club became even better known after the event, with more people visiting from abroad.

The Future of the DDC

Dewey worked on his decimal classification throughout his life, revising and updating it many times. His trusted friend May Seymour worked almost exclusively on the DDC while she was at the club. To ensure that the DDC continued to be updated and revised after his death, Dewey stipulated that all profits from the sale of each edition would be used for the publication of future editions.

and dedication to his causes brought about significant changes in several areas.

Spelling reform and metric conversion did not survive long without Dewey behind them. Today, metric conversion is often ignored. However, some federally funded construction projects are required to use metric. The scientific community also supports using the metric system, because it provides simpler and, in some cases, more accurate measurements.

But Dewey is most often remembered for his contributions to librarianship. Many of the organizations that he helped found have survived. The ALA, NYLA, *Library Journal*, and Library Bureau all continue to operate in some way. In addition, the DDC is used in libraries across the globe. First published in 1876, the DDC has been revised to include an ever-changing and ever-expanding subject matter. It has withstood the test of time.

Melvil Dewey is remembered for his contributions to libraries in the United States.

TIMELINE

1851	1868	1870
Melville Dewey is born on December 10.	Dewey saves books from a fire at the Adams Collegiate Institute. He becomes ill afterward.	Dewey enters Amherst College.

1876	1876	1876
The American Library Association is founded.	Dewey's classification system is first published.	The American Metric Bureau is formed.

1873	1874	1876
On May 8, Dewey presents his proposal for a new classification system to the Library Committee of Amherst.	Dewey changes his first name to Melvil.	The first issue of the *American Library Journal* is published.

1876	1878	1879
The Spelling Reform Association is formed.	Dewey marries Annie Roberts Godfrey on October 19.	Dewey changes his last name to Dui on his twenty-eighth birthday.

TIMELINE

1881	1883	1887
The Library Bureau is formed.	Dewey is appointed librarian-in-chief of Columbia College.	Godfrey Dewey is born on September 3.

1895	1899	1905
The Lake Placid Club is formed.	Dewey resigns as regents' secretary.	Dewey resigns as New York state librarian.

1890	1890	1892
Dewey starts work as regents' secretary and New York state librarian in Albany on January 1.	Dewey is elected president of the ALA.	Dewey is elected president of the ALA again.

1922	1924	1931
Annie Dewey dies on August 25.	Dewey marries Emily Beal on May 28.	Dewey dies on December 26.

Essential Facts

Date of Birth

December 10, 1851

Place of Birth

Adams Center, Jefferson County, New York

Date of Death

December 26, 1931

Parents

Joel and Eliza Dewey

Education

Amherst College, Massachusetts

Marriage

Annie Godfrey (October 19, 1878)
Emily Beal (May 28, 1924)

Children

Godfrey Dewey

CAREER HIGHLIGHTS

Dewey created the Dewey Decimal Classification, a comprehensive system of classifying and shelving books in libraries. In 1876, Dewey gathered fellow librarians for a conference, at which the American Library Association was founded. Dewey opened the first school for training librarians in 1887.

SOCIETAL CONTRIBUTION

More efficient libraries allow people access to educational material. Also, Dewey's advocacy of female librarians helped open the field to women.

CONFLICTS

Dewey's personality and drive to promote his causes often put him at odds with his colleagues. Dewey was forced to abandon the Readers and Writers Economy Company because of his unclear bookkeeping. He was forced to resign from his positions as regents' secretary and state librarian.

QUOTE

"The time was when a library was very much like a museum, and a librarian was a mouser in musty books, and visitors looked with curious eyes at ancient tomes and manuscripts. The time is when a library is a school, and the librarian is in the highest sense a teacher, and the visitor is a reader among the books as a workman among his tools."—*Melvil Dewey*

ADDITIONAL RESOURCES

SELECT BIBLIOGRAPHY

Battles, Matthew. *Library: An Unquiet History*. New York: W.W. Norton & Company, 2003.

Dawe, George Grosvenor. *Melvil Dewey, Seer: Inspirer: Doer*. Essex County, NY: Lake Placid Club, 1932.

Harris, Michael H. *History of Libraries in the Western World*. Metuchen, NJ: Scarecrow Press, 1995.

Rider, Fremont. *Melvil Dewey*. Chicago: American Library Association, 1994.

Vann, Sarah K. *Melvil Dewey: His Enduring Presence in Librarianship*. Littleton, CO: Libraries Unlimited, 1978.

Wiegand, Wayne A. *Irrepressible Reformer: A Biography of Melvil Dewey*. Chicago: American Library Association, 1996.

FURTHER READING

Fowler, Allan. *The Dewey Decimal System*. Chicago: Children's Press, 1997.

Lerner, Frederick Andrew. *Libraries through the Ages*. New York: Continuum, 1999.

Web Links

To learn more about Melvil Dewey, visit ABDO Publishing Company online at **www.abdopublishing.com**. Web sites about Melvil Dewey are featured on our Book Links page. These links are routinely monitored and updated to provide the most current information available.

Places to Visit

Amherst College Library
Amherst College
P.O. Box 5000
Amherst, MA 01002-5000
413-542-2000
www.amherst.edu/library
The Amherst College Library contains many reference materials and several rare collections, including historic public documents.

New York Public Library
Fifth Avenue and 42nd Street
New York, NY 10018
212-930-0800
www.nypl.org
The New York Public Library is recognized as one of the best libraries in world. Its online catalog and Web site give people all over the world access to its collections.

Glossary

acquisition
Something bought or otherwise gained for a library collection.

alumni
Graduates of a particular school.

baptism
A religious act in Christian churches that initiates a person into the community.

Baptist Church
A Protestant religious group.

classification
The process of sorting a large group of things by their similarities.

collection
A library's complete holdings.

cufflink
A decorative device that holds the cuff of a men's dress shirt closed.

faculty
The teaching staff of a school.

humility
Modesty.

inaugural
Marking the beginning of an institution, a period, or an activity.

jeopardy
To be in danger of loss or failure.

metric system
A decimal measurement system based on the meter.

papyrus
A plant from which ancient Egyptians made writing surfaces.

regent
>   An officer of a university's governing board.

resignation
>   The act of giving up a job.

stoicism
>   An indifference to pleasure or pain.

tenure
>   The period of holding an office.

trustee
>   A person who has the responsibility of controlling the administration of a property.

unabridged
>   The complete text of a work.

Source Notes

Chapter 1. Classification
1. Wiegand, Wayne A. *Irrepressible Reformer: A Biography of Melvil Dewey.*
Chicago: American Library Association, 1996. 21–22.
2. Battles, Matthew. *Library: An Unquiet History.* New York: W.W.
Norton & Company, 2003. 139.
3. Ibid. 141.

Chapter 2. A Desire to Reform
1. Wiegand, Wayne A. *Irrepressible Reformer: A Biography of Melvil Dewey.*
Chicago: American Library Association, 1996. 7.
2. Ibid. 8.

Chapter 3. The Assistant Librarian
1. Rider, Fremont. *Melvil Dewey.* Chicago: American Library
Association, 1944. 13.
2. Ibid.
3. Ibid. 18.

Chapter 4. The Year of the Library

1. Wiegand, Wayne A. *Irrepressible Reformer: A Biography of Melvil Dewey.* Chicago: American Library Association, 1996. 38.
2. Ibid.
3. Dewey, Melvil. "The Profession." *American Library Journal* 1. 1876. 5–6. Vann, Sarah K. *Melvil Dewey: His Enduring Presence in Librarianship.* Littleton, CO: Libraries Unlimited, 1978. 70–71.
4. Ibid.
5. Vann, Sarah K. *Melvil Dewey: His Enduring Presence in Librarianship.* Littleton, CO: Libraries Unlimited, 1978. 33.
6. Ibid. 32.

Chapter 5. Moving Forward

1. Wiegand, Wayne A. *Irrepressible Reformer: A Biography of Melvil Dewey.* Chicago: American Library Association, 1996. 75.
2. Rider, Fremont. *Melvil Dewey.* Chicago: American Library Association, 1944. 24.

SOURCE NOTES CONTINUED

Chapter 6. A Library School
1. Wiegand, Wayne A. *Irrepressible Reformer: A Biography of Melvil Dewey.*
Chicago: American Library Association, 1996. 80.
2. Rider, Fremont. *Melvil Dewey.* Chicago: American Library
Association, 1944. 79.

Chapter 7. The Albany Years
1. Vann, Sarah K. *Melvil Dewey: His Enduring Presence in Librarianship.*
Littleton, CO: Libraries Unlimited, 1978. 41.
2. Rider, Fremont. *Melvil Dewey.* Chicago: American Library
Association, 1944. 125.

Chapter 8. Rise and Fall
1. Rider, Fremont. *Melvil Dewey.* Chicago: American Library Association, 1944. 99–100.
2. Ibid. 100.
3. Vann, Sarah K. *Melvil Dewey: His Enduring Presence in Librarianship.* Littleton, CO: Libraries Unlimited, 1978. 49.

Chapter 9. The Last Years
1. Dewey, Melvil. "80th Birthday letr 10 Dec 31, to a fu personal frends from out Florida Branch, 7 Lakes, Lake Placid, Hylands Co, Fla." Vann, Sarah K. *Melvil Dewey: His Enduring Presence in Librarianship.* Littleton, CO: Libraries Unlimited, 1978. 226.

INDEX

ABOUT THE AUTHOR

Jill Sherman is the author of several nonfiction books for young people. She loves learning about new things and enjoys running, yoga, comic books, zombies, and television. She lives and works in New Jersey.

PHOTO CREDITS

Bettmann/Corbis, cover; David H. Lewis/iStockphoto, 6; Neil Blake/iStockphoto, 11; Melvil Dewey Papers, Rare Book and Manuscript Library, Columbia University, 13, 95; Library of Congress, 14, 19, 24, 33, 34, 43, 48, 54, 65, 69, 76, 85; Print Collection, Miriam and Ira D. Wallach Division of Art, Prints and Photographs, The New York Public Library, Astor, Lenox and Tilden Foundations, 23, 75; Corbis, 26; Courtesy American Library Association Archives (University of Illinois), record series number 99/1/14, 39, 79, 86, 88; Owen Franken/Corbis, 44; Ryan Lane/iStockphoto, 53; Frances Benjamin Johnston/Library of Congress, 57; Hulton Archive/Stringer/Getty Images, 62; Lake County Museum/Corbis, 66